# THE MAYA

Written by Richard Platt
Illustrated by Laura Tolton and Eva Morales

## CONTENTS

# RISE OF THE MAYA

Central America stretches out like a rope, tying together the two large **continents** to the north and south. People have lived here for over 20,000 years.

CENTRAL AMERICA

MEXICO

BELIZE

GUATEMALA

HONDURAS

CARIBBEAN SEA

NICARAGUA

PACIFIC OCEAN

COSTA RICA

PANAMA

SOUTH AMERICA

🌋 Volcanoes

⬤ Maya region

The people who would become the Maya travelled down from the north 9,000 years ago. They settled in the land between the Caribbean and the Pacific coasts. Some made their homes in the mountains of the south, and along the Pacific shore. Here the climate was cool and wet. Volcanoes produced the glass-like rock that the Maya used for tools.

Just north of the mountains, there was lower, gently-sloping country covered with thick tropical forests. This region was warmer and damper than the mountains, and criss-crossed by rivers. Many beasts, fish and birds darted through the water and jungle, providing lots of food for the Maya who lived here.

Farther north still were hot lowlands that were mostly drier, with no rivers. The Maya who lived here drew water from vast, deep water holes called "cenotes". Because of the heat and dryness, rough, low jungle trees grew, rather than dripping rainforest.

Today, Maya lands are mostly within Guatemala, Belize and southern Mexico.

The first people in this region didn't stay in one place. They moved around the forest hunting its wild creatures, and eating roots, leaves and berries. Gradually their lives became more settled. By 2000 BCE, most people in the region had built more permanent homes in forest clearings. They cut down trees to make fields where they could plant crops to eat.

In time, the family groups and hunting bands had time to do other things besides just farming and hunting. They used stone to create public spaces and temples.

The Maya weren't the only people here. The swampy coast of the Caribbean to the west was, for a long time, the home of the Olmec. These people built vast temples, public squares and pyramids. They're famous today for the huge portrait heads they carved from great stone boulders.

This Olmec stone head is taller than a man and weighs 24 tonnes.

To the southwest, the Zapotec people were **flourishing** in the Oaxaca valleys. They too would build a great city with spectacular stone temples, at Monte Albán.

Farther west, in what's now Mexico, there were many small cities, each controlled by a different leader. Centuries later, the Aztec people conquered this region. They ruled it from an extraordinary island city called Tenochtitlan, that's now Mexico City.

The Maya and their neighbours were alike in many ways. They prized the same hard, shiny stones such as obsidian and jade and traded them with each other. The Maya also began to trade what they made for the things they wanted.

They shared similar ways of hunting, and growing and preparing food. Their clothes, pottery and houses weren't too different in style and decoration. They spoke similar languages, and their religious beliefs and ways of worship weren't too different. They even played the same sport, using a rubber ball in a specially built court.

# Becoming the Maya

The Maya people didn't stay as scattered families, sheltering from the rain in crude jungle shelters. By 3,000 years ago, there were many more of them, and they'd divided their homeland into a patchwork of tiny kingdoms. Each one was ruled from a central town, often with grand stone **architecture**.

The time between about 250 CE and 900 CE, when the Maya cities were flourishing and the most magnificent buildings were built, archaeologists call the "Classic" Maya period.

Though most of the Maya people in the Classic period were still farmers, a few families were better off. Their houses were grander; they didn't have to work hard, and they helped organise and rule the communities where they lived. They had more possessions, collecting the beautiful things that everyone prized.

# WEALTH AND TRADE

The Maya were keen traders amongst themselves. They traded scraps of gold and copper metals, and they bought and sold finished crafts: magnificent clothing and jewellery, weapons and tools. Ordinary items, such as pottery containers, paper, dried fish and honey were also traded.

The only way to get from one city to another was on foot, for the Maya had no wheeled vehicles or animals they could ride. So traders' feet pounded a network of long-distance tracks under the jungle canopy. In parts of the Maya lands, there were paved, raised highways between cities, which made travel by foot easier and quicker.

Over 1,200 years ago, Maya cities weren't obvious to the distant traveller, as today's cities are. From far away, forest trees hid them. The shrieks of monkeys, parrots and other forest animals would have drowned out city sounds.

8

Travelling could be dangerous, for the forest also hid **predatory** animals, such as jaguars. A journey that ended safely was cause for relief and celebration. The first sign that a city was near was that planted fields replaced jungle vines. Nearby clusters of thatched houses brought the welcome smell of cooking. This meant customers for the trader and rest for the weary traveller.

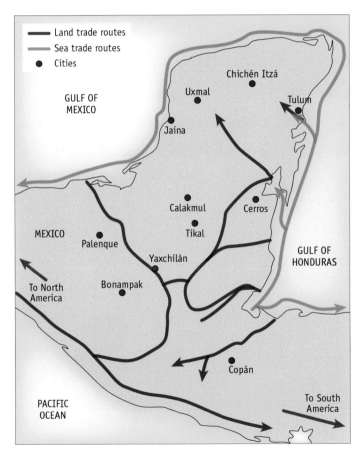

The villages that surrounded Maya cities clustered round open squares. Beyond them, the larger buildings of the city rose.

This busy, bustling world, where farmers crowded the streets and craftsmen carved stone into huge statues, was a centre of business. It would have been worth the trek through the jungle for traders to buy and sell goods. One of the most important items traders brought with them from the Pacific Coast was salt, which was used for preparing and preserving food.

There were surprises for the traveller too. From time to time, grand parades stopped not just visitors, but all traffic. Chanting priests in brilliant feathered costumes led them to the vast pyramids in the heart of the city.

For the hundreds of travellers and traders, a Maya city in 800 CE was an amazing, beautiful, exciting place.

Maya goods were also **exported** to Mexico where the Aztec people had settled. The sea was the easiest way for Maya traders to transport the beautiful luxuries they bought and sold, like colourful feathers, shells and stones – the raw materials for decoration. They travelled in large wooden canoes around the coast, from the Gulf of Honduras to the Gulf of Mexico.

How did the traders and their customers pay for what they bought and sold? The Maya didn't have coins and banknotes to exchange, as we do. If the buyer and seller each had something the other wanted, they could strike a bargain with a simple swap. If they couldn't, they used chocolate! The beans of the cocoa plant were small and easily dried. They were valuable, because the plant grew only in the mountains. Cocoa beans became the nearest thing the Maya had to money.

# LIFE IN THE COUNTRYSIDE

Though the Maya cities were very grand and exciting, most of the Maya weren't city-dwellers. They lived not far away in farming villages. Farms surrounded the cities too. Some of the farming families lived in the city's "suburbs", within walking distance of their fields.

Maya people chose farming methods that suited their forest setting. They grew just a few crops in open fields. The fields were small, because clearing land was very hard work. Farmers had only stone axes to cut down trees. On hillsides, stone walls created fields like wide steps which stopped rain washing the soil away.

Cleared land was planted with breadnut trees, and corn, squash and cotton plants. They all grew fast in the warm, damp climate. Unfortunately, wild plants grew just as quickly. Farmers spent much of their time on the back-aching task of weeding.

But fields were just a small part of Maya farming. Each family also had a garden near their home. They grew beans, hot chillies, avocado pear trees, melons and guavas. They kept the soil rich by piling on animal and human manure.

Maya people also put food on the table by hunting, and collecting plants in the forest. The forest provided flavourings for food, such as vanilla, wild mushrooms and honey. Some forest bees didn't sting, making honey collection painless.

# Meat and hunting

For meat, the Maya had as much choice as we do. Some they
raised on their farms: every family kept a few turkeys to cook
for feast days. Tame ducks ate pests from the fields until it was
their turn in the pot.

But much more of the farmer's meat came from wild animals.
**Venison** was a favourite, and farmers attracted deer by
controlling tree growth in worn-out fields. This created
the open woodland that deer prefer. Hunters also brought
home armadillos and a kind of large rat called an agouti.

Hunting was hard work because hunters had no guns. To hunt small birds, such as ducks, partridges and pigeons, they used blowpipes that fired hard clay pellets. They chased animals with the help of dogs, killing their prey with spears, clubs and knives. In later times, bows and arrows made hunting easier.

On the sea coasts, fishermen threw nets and hooks to catch fish. As well as eating them fresh, they preserved the fish in salt or by drying them. In the highlands, fishermen put a natural poison into streams that stunned fish and made them float into specially built dams, for easy collection.

Maya hunters made their spears go farther using a throwing stick called an "atlatl", which extended a hunter's arm, launching a spear with deadly speed.

# FOOD AND DRINK

Hunting was a man's job, but turning game and crops into tasty food was the work of women. It took up most of their time. **Maize** was slow to prepare. Women removed the hard shell by soaking overnight in water and lime. Then they used a stone rolling pin to crush the maize into a paste.

Flattened and shaped, the maize paste made tortillas. These tasty pancakes were cooked over a fire on a flat pottery slab. At meal times, a rolled tortilla was both food and cutlery. Without forks or spoons, it was a handy way of scooping up and eating other dishes. Some of these were meaty stews or barbecues, though meat was always scarcer than maize.

To quench their thirst, the Maya drank water flavoured with maize flour and honey. For festivals they brewed maize beer. And for a special treat, they drank chocolate. This was made from the beans of the cocoa plant, which grew only in the hills. To prepare and preserve the beans, farmers first allowed the fleshy pods in which they grew to rot in the sun, then dried the beans inside.

Besides chocolate, forest trees supplied the Maya with another sweet treat. Slashing the sapodilla tree made its sap ooze out. Boiled up, the sap hardened into a sweet, gluey mass called chicle. The Maya used it as we still do: as chewing gum.

# FABRICS AND CLOTHES

What other work did women do besides cooking? Their most important job in the home was making cloth from cotton grown in the fields. Farmers' wives and daughters twisted the fluffy cotton into long threads. Next they added colour: red dye came from a tree called Brazilwood and crushed insects; green from avocado; purple from blackberries and shellfish; and yellow from a rock.

Women wove the threads using a simple loom. One end was tied to a tree, and the other to a strap around the weaver's waist. Leaning back tightened the threads. Then the weaver could pass another thread in the over-and-under mesh that makes fabric.

The colourful textiles that women made were for trade only because dyes were costly. Fabrics for family clothes were plainer, and sewn into simple garments.

Most of the time, men wore only a strip of cloth tied round their waist and looped between their legs. In colder weather and in the hills, men wrapped themselves in a cloak, called a "pati". Women wore a length of embroidered fabric with holes for the arms and head called a "kub". On cold nights, both men and women wore deerskin moccasins and a "manta". This square of thick fabric was also useful as a blanket, and as a curtain for the house door!

# Houses

Cold days were rare in the lowlands where many of the Maya lived. So their houses had to protect them only from the heavy rain that fell between May and August. To do this, every house had a steeply sloping roof of leaves. Houses were alike in other ways. They were rectangular, and built on a low platform to keep out the forest damp. Houses surrounded small paved squares.

Each family shared a square, with young couples, their parents and their grandparents around the sides. Related families built their house groups around squares close to each other.

Houses had openings without glass for windows, and bigger openings for doorways. When a manta wasn't needed to "shut the door", a string with bells on across the doorway was enough to let the house-owner know there was a visitor.

Inside the house, a thin partition divided the sleeping area from the kitchen. The kitchen had a hole in the roof to let smoke from the fire drift out. Furniture was simple and wooden. There were tables and benches, and beds made from thin tree saplings woven together. Wooden frames kept them off the ground.

Wealthy families had bigger houses, closer to the centre of a village. In place of mud walls that needed repairs after heavy rain, they had solid stone blocks.

By making modern copies of ancient Maya homes, archaeologists have learned about their building methods and materials.

# GROWING UP MAYA

The open doors of Maya houses meant that young children were free to run in and out as they pleased. Mostly, though, they spent their time outside. The forest, garden and fields were their playground and school.

For Maya children of poor farming families, education meant watching and copying their parents. Mothers taught their daughters household tasks within the home.

Boys' schooling took place outside. Even the smallest boy could help grow food, by scaring away birds and picking off the grubs and slugs. As they got older, they learnt to sow

and harvest. Boys also learnt from their fathers how to hunt and trap animals. They skinned and gutted what they caught with a stone knife flaked as sharp as a razor.

Boys' lives were different from their sisters' in another important way too. From the age of about 12 until they married, young men slept apart from their families in a separate house. They may have learnt fighting skills here and relaxed by playing ball games.

Maya ideas of beauty were very different from ours. Cross-eyes were thought to be beautiful, and parents encouraged this by hanging a bead from a lock of hair between their child's eyes. Both eyes would focus on this bead and look cross-eyed. Older Maya – both men and women – were heavily tattooed, and their skin cut to make patterns of scars.

# Religion at home

Childhood was a dangerous stage in life. Diseases killed many children before they became adults, so their parents protected them with religion. There was a ceremony to bless each stage in a child's life. The first was a "naming" soon after birth. When children were between three and 12 years old, priests blessed groups of them. They used tobacco, holy water and incense to celebrate the event.

But religion didn't just protect children: everyone needed the help of the gods. There were lots of them – we know the names of 166 of the most important. Each controlled one part of life, so there were gods for maize, rain, sun, moon, wind, war, death and medicine. Most gods had a good and a bad side. The rain god watered crops and made them grow, but he could also cause flooding.

The Maya carved tall stones to illustrate their gods: this one is from Copán, Honduras.

The Maya even had a god of chocolate, shown here on a funeral mask. According to Maya legend, the god K'awiil discovered both maize and cocoa when he shattered a mountain with a lightning bolt and found the two plants growing inside.

At funerals, a priest wore this jade mask of K'awiil, the Maya god of lightning, snakes and maize.

As well as the gods, Maya people worshipped their ancestors: their own fathers and grandfathers, and their fathers and grandfathers before them. They were close to them in life, and kept them close in death, too, making their graves beneath their houses or just outside.

# PRIESTS AND RITUALS

For a Maya man, respecting his ancestors was a duty and a tradition. It was a painful duty, too, for it meant spilling his own blood. In a tiny family shrine close to his house, he cut his skin and smeared his blood on a **sacred** statue.

This was a private family ritual, but it was just the tiniest part of Maya worship. Public ceremonies marked every date in the Maya calendar. In celebrating these yearly festivals, numbers were crucial. A drink prepared for the new year, for example, had to be made from exactly 415 grains of maize. Other celebrations had similar strict rules. In religious dances, getting the performance just right was essential for good fortune. Drummers were punished for missing a beat.

Following the rules of religion was too difficult for ordinary village people, and to help them worship they relied on a shaman. Half priests and half wizards, shamans had special powers. They used hunger, bleeding, and they may have drunk alcohol to get in touch with the world of the gods.

Shamans were the least proud of the Maya priests. In the cities, religious rituals were grander and bigger. They were organised by specially trained priests. The Maya kings were the chief priests. Their careful worship of gods and ancestors was essential for the well-being of the city and its people.

# CITIES, SPLENDOUR AND SACRIFICE

If farmers had been the only ancient Maya people, they would have been forgotten. Long ago, jungle trees and vines grew over their muddy farms and fragile houses, leaving little trace of their lives. But, fortunately, the Maya people left behind some more lasting reminders of their power, skills and achievements: their cities. There were dozens of them, each controlling the land around. The greatest cities were huge. Tikal in Guatemala was so big it would take two hours to walk across it.

In Guatemala, the ruined city of Tikal is one of the largest that the Maya built.

Maya cities were built of gleaming white stone and covered in smooth plaster. They towered over the nearby green farm lands. The city buildings looked a little like white iced celebration cakes. Layer grew upon layer, and they narrowed from the base to the top.

Maya cities had squares, blocks of buildings, and sometimes wide, paved highways leading to neighbouring towns. But they weren't carefully planned on a grid, as many modern cities are. Around the edges, low buildings spread out in rather jumbled patterns.

The most important buildings were the tallest ones in the middle of cities. It was here that the Maya kings lived and worshipped. The buildings nearby were the setting for the colourful ceremonies that were central to Maya life.

# CITY BUILDINGS

Within the city, there were many different kinds of building.
Small temples stood at the top of the stone pyramids.
Nearby were open squares where crowds gathered to worship
and celebrate festivals. There were grand royal palaces,
and sports arenas, specially built for the hugely popular
ball games. In **observatories**, astronomers measured
the movement of the sun and stars across the sky.
And around the edges of the city, there were the beautiful
homes of the city's wealthy and important people,
and workshops for craftsmen.

At Palenque, Mexico, the
*Temple of the Cross* celebrates
the king Serpent-Jaguar, who
ruled 1300 years ago.

Triangular, shining brilliantly in the sun and topped with temples, Maya pyramids were built to impress. Even today, these great structures astonish tourists who visit them. They'd have been much more splendid 1,200 years ago when the cities were doing well. Then, brightly painted plaster smoothed off the stone steps. At the top, the temples were plastered and coloured in the same way, with towering "roof-combs". Pictures of the gods decorated these tall crests.

The Maya kings built these enormous monuments to honour and respect their dead ancestors: the earlier kings of the city. Many of the pyramids were royal tombs, and it was the duty of each king to improve and enlarge the work of his father. So pyramids were built on pyramids, on top of pyramids, in ever-growing layers.

The *Temple of the Great Jaguar* at Tikal towers 47 metres above the square below.

# BLOOD-STAINED TEMPLES

At the top of the pyramid, the Maya sacrificed prisoners of war. They smeared the blood on a statue of a god and then threw the dead body down the pyramid steps.

Human sacrifices like this were reserved for very special events, such as the **coronation** of a new king. More often Maya kings offered their own blood, as ordinary Maya people did. For kings, though, this "self-sacrifice" was a very great public event.

Using stingray spines, or special blades, Maya kings cut their skin, and let the blood flow into cups. The priests poured the blood onto pieces of paper, and then burnt the paper. By studying the smoke from the paper, the kings predicted the future.

Besides the priests, the king's ceremonies involved many assistants, musicians and dancers. Visiting kings and noblemen might have taken part. And at the foot of the pyramid, in the great square, ordinary people waited anxiously for news that the ceremony was complete, and predicted good news about the future.

# Fit for a king

Preparing for a great ceremony on the plaza or in a temple, a Maya king wore an extraordinary costume. Made of brilliantly dyed cloth, it was decorated with the feathers of rainforest birds. Over his shoulders, the king wore the skin of one of the ferocious big cats of the jungle: a jaguar. On his feet were sandals covered with rare stones. And hanging down his back he wore a stone mirror.

When first carved, this picture of the Maya king Bird-Jaguar was painted in brilliant colours.

But you might easily overlook all of this finery, because what really caught the eye was on the king's head. It was too grand to be called a hat, for it rose in the air half his height.

Expertly crafted and painted brilliant colours, it showed the king was a god.

Even on an ordinary person, this outfit would have looked astonishing, but the king was no ordinary person. The more wealthy and powerful the Maya were, the more they changed their bodies to achieve their people's ideas of beauty. So a king's teeth were filed to sharp points, his forehead was flat and high, and scars and tattoos made his skin ridged and coloured.

# Slaves and servants

To help him prepare for the solemn ceremony that was to come, a crowd of servants would have fussed around the king. Some would have been slaves who'd been captured in battle. Others may have lost their freedom through **debt**, and had become the king's possessions. But many of the king's helpers were themselves wealthy and important, for it was an honour to serve the king.

Besides helping him dress, slaves and servants prepared and served food for the king and the royal family. Like the common people of the farms and forest, Maya kings ate a lot of maize. But their diet was more mixed, as they also ate more venison than their people. Deer were hard to hunt, and the best meat was delivered to the royal palaces as a kind of taxation.
In cities near the coast, kings and other important Maya ate more fish than their people too.

Maya kings also enjoyed the luxury of hot chocolate much more often than their people could. Their servants flavoured it with chilli or vanilla. They poured it from jug to jug to make it froth like a modern cappuccino.

Scientists know what wealthy Maya people ate in two ways. First, they've studied the **middens** of both rich and poor Maya people.

Human bones provide a clue, too. Diet changes the chemicals stored in human bones, so by analysing skeletons, it's possible to work out what people ate.

Painted on a vase, this woman servant is offering the king a drink – probably foaming hot chocolate.

# LIVING LIKE A GOD

You might say that Maya kings lived like gods, but you'd be wrong. For Maya kings *were* gods, and their people worshipped them. Why were they so admired?

Maya kings were special and holy because their fathers – and their grandfathers before them – were special and holy. There was another reason, too: they had special powers. In the public rituals they performed, they had visions and saw into the future. By cutting their bodies and spilling their blood, they pleased the gods. And by leading their soldiers in warfare, they made their kingdoms great and powerful.

Most Maya rulers were men, but not all of them. Experts know of at least five Maya queens. They usually gained power when a king died without a son. This is how Lady Yohl Ik'nal became queen, and ruled Palenque for more than 20 years from 583 CE.

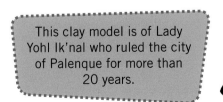

This clay model is of Lady Yohl Ik'nal who ruled the city of Palenque for more than 20 years.

# STRANGE HOME FOR A KING

When their blood-gifts in the temples were complete, Maya kings returned to their palaces. They were different from royal palaces anywhere else in the world. Instead of soaring ceilings and wide open halls, Maya palaces were cramped, narrow spaces. Their architects and builders didn't use wide arches. They supported roofs and ceilings with solid columns that grew gradually closer as they rose. This made rooms tall, with inward-sloping walls.

As well as this tall tower, the palace at Palenque had luxurious baths and a sauna.

Archaeologists who've studied the Maya palaces argue over just how the kings lived in them. There were no bedrooms or kitchens. How did the royal family sleep? Where was their food prepared? Archaeologists can only guess. Maybe the "palaces" were just for ceremonies, and the kings lived in wooden buildings that have since rotted away. Perhaps – like their people – kings spent more time outdoors, in the large courtyards next to their palaces.

There are mysterious clues carved in stone in the courtyards themselves. For in front of each palace there was a "stela". This tall slab of beautifully carved stone stood above a round stone altar. Some were huge: three times the height of an adult. The carvings show finely dressed men holding strange objects, or warriors crushing their foes. Carved writings identify the figures and date the monuments.

A Maya stone stela. Royal artists were sometimes responsible for carving the stone.

# A WHOLE NEW BALL GAME

There's less mystery about the ball-courts. These were long, wide playing fields with walls on either side. The largest court that still survives is at the city of Chichén Itzá. It's the length of six tennis courts and about a third as wide.

Within this court, Maya teams played a game called pok-a-tok. Even the name sounds like the echoing sound of a ball bouncing between two flat walls. The ball was as big as a small melon, but it was solid rubber, so it weighed up to four kilogrammes. A ball this heavy could cause serious injuries, so players wore gloves and a U-shaped wooden belt to protect their waists.

Players could hit the ball only with their fists, elbows and bottoms. They aimed to knock the ball through a stone ring set high on the walls of the court. This happened only rarely. In a similar game played in Mexico, the player who hit the ball through the ring could claim the clothes and jewellery of all the spectators!

There was a scary side to pok-a-tok. Carvings at some ball courts show winning players holding up the cut-off heads of their opponents. For pok-a-tok was warfare acted out as a game, and the losers sometimes paid with their lives.

As well as ordinary Maya people, ball-game players included important noblemen and perhaps even the king himself.

# OFFICIALS

Maya city-kingdom society wouldn't have worked without the help of officials. The greatest of these were in charge of a large area. Less important officials helped them, or governed villages. They collected taxes, which the farmers paid in food, and by working, and made sure that everyone obeyed the law.

These officials led comfortable lives in fine homes. They had better food than the farmers and shared some of the luxuries that the king and his family enjoyed.

So too did the priests. Maya priests did much more than organise worship. Today we'd say that they did the work of mathematicians, **scribes** and astronomers.

A codex was a folding book written by Maya priests to record knowledge or religious rituals.

The homes, offices and schools of these fortunate people were crowded round the palaces and temples of the city, or were at the centre of villages.

# CRAFTS AND ART

Not all of those in the city worked with their brains like
the officials. In workshops near the centre, artists and craft-
workers kept their hands busy with paint, feathers, fabrics,
mats and baskets. From their workshops came beautiful objects
for the pleasure of their rulers, for trade, or for day-to-day use.

Much of their work has rotted in the steamy jungle climate.
But experts know of these crafts from descriptions from early
Spanish explorers and surviving carved pictures. Feather-work
was the most colourful. Artists glued or tied feathers on to
capes and headdresses. The feathers came from trapped jungle
birds, or from caged birds kept just for their feathers.

The most beautiful feather-
work, made from the
shining green tail of the
quetzal bird, was reserved
for the king. Anyone who
killed or caught a quetzal
without permission was
executed!

Few scraps of Maya fabrics have survived, but we know from paintings that it had bright colours and striped patterns. People in the region still weave very similar cloth. Mats and baskets have all rotted. Archaeologists know details of them from where they were pressed into mud, preserving their patterns when it hardened.

Maya painters' work has survived better. Paint soon flaked where the rain and sun struck it, but buried paintwork survived. When archaeologists dug up a tomb from Xultún, a city hidden for more than ten centuries, they found walls painted with fantastic colourful scenes.

# Pottery and stone

Crafts made in hard materials, such as stone and pottery, have survived better. Maya stoneworkers created some of the most detailed and beautiful objects ever made from stone.

Making stone axes and knives for everyday use was probably a common skill. But only expert craftsmen could make amazing shapes out of a hard stone called flint, which were carefully chipped out to look like human figures, or just pleasing patterns. Stoneworkers also carved hard green jadeite stone into small sculptures and pictures – all without metal tools. They cut and drilled the stone using cords and sticks covered in a grinding paste of sand and water.

Maya potters produced a vast range of styles. The simplest were plain cooking pots, but they also made pots painted in many colours with lifelike scenes. As they perfected their potting skills, the Maya set up pot factories with moulds to speed production. By coating the pots with a **mineral** called talc, they even gave them a non-stick surface!

# READING AND WRITING

Open a Mayan book and you won't see writing as you understand it. Instead, there are pictures of Maya people and gods, crouching or standing. Around them are detailed, rounded-off signs, each no bigger than a fingernail, with bold lines and dots.

These signs are hieroglyphs – a kind of picture-writing. Many of the hundreds of signs stand for a whole word. A few look like the thing they are describing. For example, "to sow" looks like a hand scattering seed. But a few of the signs stand for sounds, like **syllables** in English, for example:

to sow    to grab    "bi"    "ye"

man    ten    to die

The Maya weren't the only people in the world to develop a writing system like this. Egyptian writing worked the same way. However, no other Central American people had a written language.

Some of what we know about the Maya today comes from their books, called codexes. Very few codexes have survived, but fortunately the Maya didn't just write on paper. Experts have learnt much more from their stone monuments. Craftsmen carved and moulded hieroglyphs all over them. The signs let everyone know which king or god they honoured, and the date they were built.

# THE CALENDAR AND ASTRONOMY

The Maya measured dates in years, just like we do, but their calendar was more complex than ours. In fact, they had not one calendar, but five!

The first one, called the "haab" was like our calendar. It was based on the Sun's movement, so that the seasons came round in the same month each year.

The second was a sacred calendar, with 20 months, each 13 days long. The third calendar was called the "long count". It measured the number of haab years that had passed since Maya time began, in 3113 BCE.

The other two calendars were based on regular changes in the night sky. The Moon calendar traced the Moon's changing phases. The last calendar of the five was based on Venus. This planet wanders among the stars. It returns to the same place roughly every 19¾ months.

Maya calendars were drawn up and controlled by priests who were also astronomers.

Calendars were important to the Maya priests, because dates ruled their religious festivals. Their knowledge also allowed them to predict eclipses, when the Sun, Moon and Earth line up in the sky. Eclipses turn day into night, or make the Moon blood-red. By predicting them, priests appeared to control the Sun itself – which would have been an awesome and frightening skill to ordinary Maya people.

This huge stone disc, 3.5 metres across, shows the Aztec calendar.

# COUNTING AND NUMBERS

To count and write down dates and numbers, the Maya had a system of dots and bars. They drew a shell shape to represent the number zero. They used this important counting idea 11 centuries before Europeans understood it.

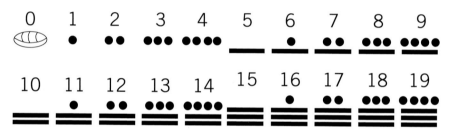

Despite the Maya's astonishing scientific abilities, they never developed important technology that we rely on. How did they manage? They didn't have wheels or tame animals to do the hard work for them. They divided heavy loads into bundles small enough for one person to carry. The heaviest weights, such as stones weighing as much as 65 tonnes, they dragged on the ground.

They lacked metal, but they became expert at making tools from stone. By striking a piece of stone at just the right angle, they made disposable blades that were sharper than any metal knife.

# FIGHTING FOR THE CITY

With all these skilled craftspeople, officials and amazing architecture, cities were worth defending.

A Maya warrior would have been a terrifying sight. His skin was painted black and red, and a tunic of jaguar skin protected his chest. On his head, he wore a scary, tall headdress. When he attacked, he let out a hideous war cry. Behind him, thumping war drums and shrill whistles from shell-trumpets helped spread fear among the enemy.

Though they didn't have guns, Maya warriors carried weapons that could easily kill. They hurled spears that had been hardened in fires or tipped with stone. They fired darts from blow-guns, and threw stones from slings. As they drew closer to their foe, they swung stone clubs and axes edged with sharpened stone. To protect themselves against attack, warriors wore cotton armour stiffened with salt, and carried long leather shields.

# PRISONERS AS PRIZES

The enemy were usually the soldiers of a neighbouring city-state. For the Maya were constantly at war with each other.

To the Maya, war was a kind of game – but a bloody and deadly serious one. Its main purpose was to take prisoners for sacrifice at ceremonies in the victor's city.

Noble prisoners were the most highly prized: taking a prisoner brought respect, and the more important the captive, the greater the respect. Less important captives faced a different fate from the nobles. Instead of being sacrificed they were made slaves or servants, and some were even adopted as family members!

Taking prisoners for sacrifice wasn't the only reason why the Maya fought each other. They also aimed to destroy their enemies' important buildings such as temples, and to force the enemy to pay tribute to them.

The attacks on neighbouring Maya cities weren't like modern warfare. The warriors included the city's most important people – often the king himself fought. Battles were small, with just a few hundred people fighting on each side. Cities were between a two- and eight-day march apart, and warriors had to carry everything they needed for battle.

The greatest achievement for any warrior was to capture a king. For the defeated city, this was a disaster. A new ruler couldn't take power until the old one had died. When warriors from Tonina captured the king of rival city Palenque in 711 CE, they kept him as a prisoner for ten years. The defeated city was without a leader for all that time.

As the number of Maya people grew, wars between city-states changed. Instead of being a ritual for taking captives, it became a struggle for land. Wars got bigger and were more destructive. People began to build walls around their city to defend themselves from attack. And some historians even believe that war may have helped bring an end to the Maya world.

# COLLAPSE!

For over 1,000 years, the Maya built wonderful cities, and covered the region they lived in with rich farming villages. Yet in the 8th and 9th centuries, these proud people left their cities. Jungle vines quickly covered the ruined monuments and abandoned farms. What could have caused this disaster?

Archaeologists argue about the reasons for the "Maya collapse". But it seems likely that overcrowding and climate change ended Maya glory.

Maya farmers worked hard to make the most of their fields, forests and gardens. They were able to feed many people from small areas of land. But when the number of families grew, farmers found it difficult to provide enough food. Turning more forest into fields didn't help: heavy rain washed away the thin soil. By the 8th century, the Maya were struggling to feed all their people.

Then the climate changed. Central America got drier. The rains that watered the forest and the crops became unreliable. Forest trees grew more slowly. Animals that once roamed the forests in large numbers got harder to find and hunt.

A terrible drought left the land parched and useless in 810 CE. The same thing happened again 50 and 100 years later. Each time, crops withered in the fields. The Maya people starved.

# THE END

Experts don't know exactly how the end came, but perhaps poor Maya farmers rebelled against their rulers. The ceremonies that priests promised would keep the rain falling no longer worked. So the taxes and luxuries the kings and their families demanded dried up.

Once their god-like powers had gone, Maya rulers fled their cities. Weeds, then trees, grew in the ball-courts. **Squatters** moved into the palaces and made the temples into rubbish dumps.

Some cities survived for longer than others. The collapse was quickest in the southern lowlands. The northern lowland cities continued to thrive for a couple more centuries. But by the end of the 15th century, the once-great Maya civilisation was gone. The old Maya kingdoms remained, but their cities were in ruins. The great traditions, temples, and craftsmanship were just a memory.

Scientists have found clues to the Maya collapse in ocean mud!
Measuring how much titanium metal was in each layer gave
them a rainfall calendar. Heavy rain washes titanium from
the land, so smaller amounts show a drought.

Woodworking tells a story of rainforest destruction.
Builders preferred straight, easily carved timber from
the sapodilla tree, but supplies ran out. After 741 CE, temple
builders in the city of Tikal switched to logwood, which has
a small, hard-to-carve trunk.

The ruins of Palenque were discovered in 1746.

# WARLIKE VISITORS ARRIVE

European people knew nothing of the Maya – or of any American peoples – until 600 years ago. But from 1492, explorers from Southern Europe began to make the first voyages across the central Atlantic to the Caribbean. Twenty-five years later, Spanish soldiers and sailors reached the coasts of Maya lands. More expeditions followed.

These first European visitors weren't like today's friendly tourists.

They didn't harmlessly explore the strange and colourful "New World" they'd discovered. Instead they were seeking treasure. They were greedy to grab whatever they could. Wherever they went, they planted their flags and claimed the land as Spanish. They were called "conquistadors", the Spanish word for conquerors.

In 1519, a Mexican described the Spanish conquistadors' greed for treasure: "The truth is that they longed and lusted for gold."

The Spanish also brought with them priests and monks, who were keen to spread the Christian religion. The blood-soaked ceremonies of the Maya and their Mexican Aztec neighbours horrified them. They called the Central American people "savages". The priests were determined to convert the Maya to Christianity – even if this meant killing those who followed a different religion.

# METALS AND GUNPOWDER

Conquering the Maya should have been easy. The Spanish had powerful and deadly weapons that the Maya lacked. They had long, sharp steel swords and powerful crossbows. They wore metal armour to protect themselves against Maya weapons. They had guns and cannons that could kill from a distance of a kilometre. They fought from horses that could out-run Maya warriors.

They also had an invisible weapon: disease. The Maya had no natural resistance to European illnesses such as **smallpox**. Hundreds of thousands died from infections that spread through the region.

What's more, the Spanish were cunning. They worked out that the Maya had a long history of fighting each other. The Spanish made the most of the Maya's hatred. They formed **alliances** with kings to defeat neighbouring cities. When they were victorious, the Spanish betrayed their Maya allies. They killed their leaders and burnt their cities.

Finally, the Spanish were helped by the predictions of some Maya priests. They'd foretold that strangers with white beards would arrive and would become gods. The Spanish fitted that description, and in places they were welcomed and worshipped.

Though the Maya fought bravely, their stone-edged clubs were no match for the Spaniards' metal swords.

# THE MAYA FIGHT BACK

Despite these advantages, the Spanish struggled to conquer the Maya. Just to reach the great cities, they had to hack their way through dense jungle. When battles began, the Maya warriors didn't fight them as the Spanish expected. Instead they fought like modern **guerrillas**. They carried out ambushes and surprise attacks, or crept up on their enemies at night.

Conquest had been quicker in central Mexico. There the whole country fell to the Spanish once they defeated its Aztec rulers. But the Maya had no single king or emperor. The conquistadors had to fight each small kingdom in turn.

The Spanish didn't control much of the Maya lands until 1542. Even after their defeat was complete, the Maya never really submitted to Spanish rule. Rebellions flared up again and again into the 20th century.

Their defeat by the Spanish changed the Maya way of life forever – and not for the better. They were forced to settle in new towns. They could neither grow crops in the way they had before, nor hunt and gather wild food. The farming methods that the Spanish introduced weren't suitable for the forest. They turned much of the region to wasteland where nothing grew.

The Spanish overlords forced Christianity on to the Maya, and their priests were tortured and killed. The Spanish burnt precious Maya books – only three or four survived.

# MAYA REDISCOVERED

During the Spanish conquest, a few priests and officials took an interest in the Maya way of life. They carefully wrote down the details of their language, beliefs, traditions and religion. Most of these accounts lay forgotten on dusty library shelves in Spain. In Central America, the ruined Maya cities had disappeared under jungle leaves.

But then, in the late 18th century, rumours began to spread about the extraordinary remains of Maya cities, especially Palenque. When the rumours reached the King of Spain, he sent expeditions to Central America to search for the ruins. In 1822, Spanish artist, Ricardo Alméndariz, brought back from the jungle the first drawings of Palenque.

American writer, John Lloyd Stephens, read reports of the Spanish expeditions, and he was fascinated. He went to Central America in 1839 to work for his government. There he travelled to Maya lands with artist Frederick Catherwood. Together they explored many of the Maya cities. Published in books, their descriptions and vivid pictures sparked huge interest in the "lost jungle cities".

John Stephens even bought a whole Maya city for $50. A local landowner sold it because it was too rocky to farm.
The American writer-explorer wanted to take the city apart and transport it to the USA to show in a museum.

While he sketched, artist Frederick Catherwood wore gloves and a net over his head to keep away the stinging insects and mosquitoes.

To help him draw subjects like the carved head of Itzamná, Catherwood used a lens which projected the scene on to his sketch pad.

# ARCHAEOLOGY BEGINS

Scientific studies of the Maya and their world began at the end of the 19th century. British archaeologist, Alfred Maudslay, and German-Italian explorer, Teobert Maler, started it. They cleared the forest trees and vines from the ruins. They photographed and mapped them, and made casts of carvings by pressing squashy wet paper over them and taking an impression.

Alfred Maudslay first visited the Maya lands to study birds, returning ten years later to explore and record the ruins.

While archaeologists dug in Maya lands, **scholars** were at work in libraries. Studying the few remaining Maya books and pictures of carved writing, they puzzled over the language and calendar. It was a very long and difficult process. The first signs to be translated, about a century ago, were about numbers, **astronomy** and the calendar. By the 1980s, language experts could understand three-quarters of Mayan hieroglyphs.

These mostly recorded the lives of wealthy, important Maya. However, modern archaeology tells us how ordinary Maya people lived. In the 1960s, American scientists carefully mapped the low house platforms around the city of Tikal. They showed that Maya cities could be huge, with homes for more than 50,000 people.

Today, archaeologists studying the Maya still hack their way through jungle creepers in the heat. But modern technology guides them to ruins. **NASA** satellites can see through clouds and forest leaves to pick out cities that have been lost for centuries.

Computer processing of satellite images changes the colours of the forest to reveal the buildings in bright yellow.

# THE MAYA PEOPLE TODAY

The Maya people didn't just vanish when the Spanish conquered them. Many fiercely resisted Spanish rule. And most of them tried to hold on to their old ways of life. They taught their children the ancient traditions, language and religion.

Today, there are seven million Maya people living in Guatemala, Belize, Mexico, Honduras and El Salvador. Most speak a form of the Mayan language, but also understand and speak Spanish.

Many of those who are Christians also still follow the religion of their ancestors. Maya traditions which celebrate the planting and harvesting of crops are especially popular.

On the steps of a church in Guatemala Maya people sell flowers.

There are important lessons to be learnt from the Maya, and the collapse of their way of life. As their numbers grew, the Maya found it harder and harder to get enough food and water for everyone. They ran out of the precious plants and trees their ancestors had used for centuries.

Today, we can see the same pattern all over the Earth, as the rising population threatens the natural resources everyone relies on.

The final blow from which the Maya never recovered was climate change. Lack of rain made it impossible to continue with their way of living. Now we all face a similar threat, and unless we learn from the Maya, our own society may collapse as theirs did.

# GLOSSARY

**alliances**    agreements between different groups of people

**architecture**    buildings that have been specially designed

**astronomy**    the study of the universe beyond the Earth

**BCE**    before the common era (the same as BC)

**CE**    common era (the same as AD)

**continents**    the Earth's seven largest areas of land

**coronation**    ceremony when a king or queen is crowned

**debt**    owing something to another person

**exported**    sent to another country to sell

**flourishing**    growing strong and healthy

**guerrillas**    groups of soldiers who make surprise attacks

**humble**    not proud

**maize**    a type of corn with yellow grain

**middens**    rubbish dumps where remains like bones and human excrement can be found

**mineral**    a substance in the earth, that doesn't come from a plant or animal

**NASA**    National Aeronautics and Space Administration, an organisation in the USA for space research and travel

**observatories**    buildings with equipment for studying the sun, moon, stars and planets

**predatory**    hunting, killing and living on the flesh of other animals

**sacred**    connected to religion

**scholars**    students who research and study

**scribes**    writers and readers

**smallpox**    a disease that caused fever and pus-filled spots

**squatters**    people who occupy land or buildings that don't belong to them

**syllables**    parts of a word with one vowel sound

**venison**    deer meat

# INDEX

# THE RISE AND FALL OF